I0471078

Estate Planning For Authors

by Gin Jones

Estate Planning For Authors

Gin Jones

First Edition

ISBN 978-1490405445

Copyright 2013 Gin Jones

This ebook is licensed for your personal enjoyment only. This ebook may not be re-sold or given away to other people, in whole or in part. If you would like to share this book with another person, please purchase an additional copy for each recipient. If you're reading this book and did not purchase it, or it was not purchased for your use only, then please return to your favorite book retailer and purchase your own copy. Thank you for respecting the hard work of the author.

http://www.thewritegin.blogspot.com

Table of Contents

Estate Planning For Authors

by Gin Jones

Introduction

Have you ever thought about what will happen to your stories after you're gone? You may know your copyright will likely continue for seventy years after your death, but have you considered what that really means? Do you know what you want to happen with your literary works after you're gone? Do you have any ideas about who could manage them for you and your heirs? And if so, have you executed the documents necessary to make sure your wishes are carried out?

None of us likes to dwell on our own mortality.

Fantasy author Neil Gaiman summarized the basic situation in his blog, where he wrote that we "secretly believe we're going to live forever and that making a will would mean letting Death in a crack."

Over the course of a decade as a practicing attorney, I heard all the excuses for not wanting to do an estate plan. Everyone is a little nervous when talking about mortality, and many people also get nervous around lawyers or when dealing with things that are new and perhaps a little foreign to them, like the legal technicalities of wills and estate planning. Authors have an extra disincentive to make plans for their estates: many of us don't believe enough in the future value of our assets (especially as-yet unpublished manuscripts) to protect them.

Being nervous is perfectly understandable. You were probably nervous before you wrote your first story or sent it off to a publisher, or hit "publish" at the digital retailer of your choice. It's time to get over whatever's stopping you, and do what's necessary to protect your literary assets. You don't hesitate to protect your other valuable assets. You buy insurance, you keep them in as safe a location as possible, and you do the necessary maintenance on them.

The purpose of this book is to give you the information that will make estate planning less scary, so you will treat your literary assets with as much care as you give all of your other valuable possessions.

Disclaimer

This book is intended for educational purposes, to assist you in understanding the basics of legal issues for authors. It is not intended to take the place of personalized advice from a knowledgeable lawyer, accountant or financial planner qualified to practice in the jurisdiction where you live and work, and does not create an attorney-client relationship. I strongly recommend consulting with a professional after reading this book and before implementing your estate plans, to be sure that they comply with local variations in the law and are consistent with your individual situation. Further, unless otherwise stated, any tax advice contained herein is not intended or written to be used, and cannot be used, by the recipient to avoid any federal tax penalty that may be imposed on the recipient or to promote, market, or recommend to another any referenced entity, investment plan or arrangement.

Chapter 1: Overview of estate planning

The basic purpose of estate planning is to make sure that your assets are managed according to your wishes, even after you are no longer able to manage them yourself. The very first topic you need to consider, then, is the big picture: how should your literary assets be managed in the future?

You've probably already made this decision with respect to many of your other assets, even if you didn't think of it as estate planning, since it didn't involve executing a will. If you own a home, and the title is held jointly with a spouse, life partner or other family member, the choice of how to hold title is a form of estate planning. If you have a 401(k) account or life insurance policy, and you've named a beneficiary, the designation of a beneficiary is a form of estate planning. If you don't have a will, that inaction is itself a form of estate planning, since your state has laws that determine who will get the assets of anyone who dies without a will.

Many people are perfectly okay with the default priorities, set by their state, for who gets an estate's assets. Those laws were drafted, after all, with an eye to what most people would want to happen, distributing the assets among the closest family members. The problem for authors is that these laws aren't particularly good at dealing with copyright, as we'll see in Chapter 6.

The first step in an estate plan is to decide what you care about. The possible goals for an estate plan generally fall into three categories: control, simplicity, and cost.

You've probably heard about the Triple Constraint, which states that for any project or purchase there are three basic options: cheap, fast or good, and you are only likely to get two of those three. In order to buy something cheaply and quickly, you may need to sacrifice quality. If you care more about quality, and still want speed, the price is not going to be cheap.

The same basic rule applies to the options in estate planning: control, ease and cost minimization. You can create a plan that gives you a great deal of control over what happens to your assets, a plan that makes the disposition of your assets easy, or a plan that minimizes costs (including legal fees, probate fees and taxes). It's not difficult to create a plan that does two of those three, but it's highly unlikely that you will be able to attain all three.

What is your highest priority? You may wish to maintain significant control over your assets, even after your death, or you may trust your heirs to do what's right, despite the risk that it won't be what you'd have chosen. You may wish to have the simplest possible estate plan, or you may prefer a slightly more complicated one that gives you more control and that minimizes risks. You may wish to keep costs to an absolute minimum, even if there are some risks of things going wrong, or you may be more flexible with respect to the costs, if you can be sure that your wishes will be followed and the distribution of assets will happen smoothly.

We'll get into your options in greater detail later, but for now, just start thinking about your priorities: control, simplicity or cost. Which of them would you compromise, to gain more from the other two? There's no right or wrong answer here, just different answers that fit different personalities and different circumstances.

Chapter 2: How does probate work?

The history of probate procedures.

You may have read *Bleak House*, Dickens's tale of never-ending litigation over an estate, or you may have heard about the various delays and expenses of probate court. Or you may simply have read the ads offering to help you avoid probate, and concluded (as the advertisers intended you to) that probate court was a house of horrors, to be avoided at all costs.

There is, of course, some truth to Dickens's fiction and the various anecdotes about probate court. But it's not the whole story, and it shouldn't be the sole basis for your decisions about your own estate. Let's start with the basics of how probate works, so you can decide for yourself.

Historically, as the Dickens novel demonstrates, probate rules were highly technical and time-consuming. Recently, there's been a trend toward simplification, while still maintaining the most basic safeguards for ensuring that the correct heirs receive the estate's assets.

In 1969, the National Conference of Commissioners on Uniform State Laws drafted a Uniform Probate Code for consideration by the individual states. The intent was to help states to simplify their procedures as well as to encourage uniformity from state to state. Having fifty wildly different procedures wasn't a problem at a time when state residents lived in one place for their entire lives, but it can lead to confusion and poor estate planning in the more mobile society we have today.

To date, only about half of the U.S. states have adopted some version of the Uniform Probate Code, but it is likely that more states will follow suit over time. About half of the states have adopted it. For simplicity's sake, I will be using the terminology and basic procedures used in the Uniform Probate Code in this book. You will, of course, be seeking professional advice before executing your own estate plan, and that professional will be able to tell you what your own state's procedures are. Until then, if you would like to read the Uniform Probate Code for yourself, or see if it's been adopted in your state, you can find that information here: http://uniformlaws.org/Act.aspx?title=Probate%20Code .

Note, however, that "uniform" is a relative term, since many states have made some modifications to the text in the course of adopting it. Even if your state has adopted the uniform code, you can't rely on the wording of the proposed code, but should check the actual text as adopted by your state.

Basic procedure today.

The basic procedure for probating an estate has six basic steps: a petition for probate is filed with the court, the court appoints a personal representative (sometimes referred to as an executor or administrator), the personal representative then "marshals the assets" (identifies and exercises control over the assets), determines the extent of valid claims against the estate (identifies the outstanding debts), prepares an accounting, and then pays the debts and distributes the net assets. There may be a seventh step in large estates, consisting of the filing of an estate tax return. (See Chapter 8 below.)

If there are no complications, such as a will contest, improper delays by the personal representative, or a tax audit, the entire probate procedure can be completed in about eighteen months. A more complicated estate, which may involve courtroom squabbles among the heirs, a pending lawsuit by or against the estate, or assets not easily transferred, can take three to five years, but very rarely the multiple generations of *Bleak House.* The longer the process takes, however, the more expenses are likely to be incurred, reducing the amount of the final distributions.

The petition for probate sets out the name of the person who died (the "decedent"), the date of death, whether there is a will, and the names and contact information of the decedent's heirs (family members and anyone else mentioned in the will). The petition is signed by the person who is seeking appointment as the personal representative of the estate. Some probate codes still use the historic terms for this role: an "executor" (male) or "executrix" (female) in cases where there is a will, and an "administrator" (male) or "administratrix" (female) in cases where there is no will. The general trend, however, follows the Uniform Probate Code, substituting the neutral term, "personal representative."

The Uniform Probate Code has a priority list for who can request appointment as the personal representative. The first choice is whoever is nominated for the position in a will, if there is a valid will. If there is no will, or the persons named in the will are unwilling or unable to accept the appointment, the Code sets out a fairly common-sense hierarchy, essentially starting with the surviving spouse, then beneficiaries of the will and other family members, and finally a public administrator. Note that anyone in the hierarchy who is not an adult under the relevant state's laws, or who is not mentally competent will be precluded from serving as personal representative.

The typical pattern for most clients is to designate the spouse to be the personal representative, and then provide that if the spouse is unavailable, the client's sibling, friend or adult child will become the personal representative. In some situations, when the estate is extremely small or straightforward, the personal representative may be able to file all the necessary papers and transfer all the assets without legal representation or financial advice. More often, what happens is that the named personal representative hires an attorney who specializes in probate practice to do the actual work. The personal representative makes any decisions with respect to matters that are within the representative's discretion, and the attorney makes sure those decisions are carried out.

An author's estate may pose some additional challenges for the personal representative, which may affect your choice of a personal representative. These issues will be discussed in detail in Chapter 6. For now, though, jot down your initial thoughts about who you'd like to name as your first and second choices for your personal representative. If you have a trusted financial advisor or legal advisor, and would like your personal representative to work with them, make a note of their names and contact information too.

Chapter 3: What are your probate assets?

Inventory of assets.

In order to make sure that your assets are managed according to your wishes, both you and the person drafting your will need to have at least a general snapshot of what your assets are.

Assets fall into two basic categories: real estate and personal property.

Real estate is land and buildings and everything attached to the land (*e.g.*, the built-in cabinets and the plumbing and the shed and the in-ground pool and the driveway and the trees). It doesn't matter if it's in the form of a condo or a single-family residence or a commercial building. If it's land or a structure (or a part of a structure), it's real estate.

Personal property is everything else. Personal property, in turn, is broken into two subcategories: tangible and intangible property. Tangible personal property is anything (other than real estate) that you can touch: your furniture, your computer, your gold coin collection, the print-out of your manuscript. Intangible property is anything you cannot touch: the value of your bank account and other investments, the copyright on your manuscript, and your contracts (e.g., the contract with a trade publisher, or the contract you enter into by listing a self-published book with a retailer). For more on copyright generally, and the complications that ownership of copyrights may present for an estate, see Chapter 6 below.

For estate planning purposes, you don't need a detailed inventory of the sort that might be useful for a homeowner's or renter's insurance policy, which lists every piece of furniture and carpet and pair of socks. (Although, if you do have that sort of inventory, it's a great starting point for thinking about your estate plan.) You do need a basic idea of what assets you own.

Start with the usual things that most people have: house/condo, valuable furniture, vehicles, stock, bank accounts, electronics, jewelry, tools and art. Jot down a brief description and where the items are located (*e.g.*, in the home, or in a safe deposit box).

Next, add the items that are unique to authors: contracts with publishers/retailers, copyrights, trademarks (if any), and pen names. Make sure to include all of your online assets, which may consist of PayPal balances or accounts payable from online retailers (profits or royalties earned but not yet paid), plus social networks, blogs, domain names, websites, Twitter accounts and whatever comes next in the virtual world. Just as you indicated where the tangible property was located, make a note of where these items are located, by noting the URLs and user names. You may also want to indicate where you store the passwords for these accounts, as long as you will be able to keep this list in a secure place.

Once you have a complete list of your valuable assets, go back and indicate a current market value for each of them. Don't stress too much over the valuation, just give it your best shot. Accurate valuation for probate and tax purposes is beyond the scope of this book, and not necessary for planning purposes. Assigning an approximate value to the assets, however, will help you to make decisions in the planning process. This list can also be invaluable if you keep it with your will, since it will help your personal representative carry out his or her duties.

Even though you don't need to establish exact valuations, do be reasonable. Your writings are all priceless in your eyes, but that doesn't help your personal representative figure out what to do with them. If you have a story that's been selling one copy a day for the past year, with every indication that it will continue at that slow but steady rate for the foreseeable future, then you might start with a value that's equal to your profit for a year's worth of sales. On the other hand, if you have a story that's consistently selling 100 copies a day on average, with no signs of dropping off, then you might value it at your per-copy profit times 100 copies a day times 365 days (or however many days you think it's likely to continue selling at that rate). If you have a book that briefly sold a thousand copies a day, but then dropped down to one a day, and spiked again with each new release, you need to acknowledge the fact that once you're gone, there won't be any new releases, so there won't be any more spikes, so the value will more likely continue at the one-a-day rate, rather than the thousand-a-day rate. You don't need to explain your math to your legal adviser or your personal representative, although you can if you wish. The bottom line is just to give your legal adviser and personal representative an idea of the relative value of each asset.

When you've assigned a value to each asset, make sure to indicate the date of the valuation. Ideally, it will be many years from now before your estate is probated, and the personal representative will need to factor in the amount of time that's passed since you assigned values to the assets.

Probate assets and non-probate assets.

Your personal representative will need to know the full extent of your assets, even though some of them will not be controlled by the probate court. You should also be aware of the distinction between probate assets (assets that are subject to the probate court's control) and non-probate assets, so that you understand how the terms of your will be applied to your assets.

Note: the laws defining property ownership vary from state to state, and may involve slightly different terminology. Make sure to check with a legal adviser in your jurisdiction for the correct terminology and definitions that apply to your assets.

The distinction between probate and non-probate assets has nothing to do with the type of asset (*e.g.*, real versus personal; bank accounts versus stock versus motor vehicles), but is determined by the form of ownership. For probate purposes, there are basically four forms of ownership: individual, joint, tenants in common and life estate.

As a general rule, individual ownership, just as the description implies, is when one person owns an item. For example, if your house or your car or your bank account is in your name alone, that's individual ownership. Items that are owned individually, by just one person, are probate assets.

Joint ownership (sometimes written as "joint with the right of survivorship" or abbreviated to "joint WROS") is when an item is owned by two or more individuals, with the proviso that when one owner dies, the remaining owner(s) automatically gets the deceased owner's share. A common example is when your car or house is owned jointly with a spouse, and the title or deed specifies that you are owning it as joint tenants or as tenants by the entirety (a joint tenancy when the parties are married to each other). Joint ownership is a non-probate asset, since the property goes to the survivor more or less automatically, without any ruling by the probate court. (Note, however, that there may be other actions that need to be taken to clear the title, such as filing or recording a death certificate. These actions will not be taken in the probate court, but will generally be done in the appropriate registry of motor vehicles or registry of deeds.)

Tenants in common is another form of ownership whereby more than one person holds title to an asset, except in this case, when one of the owners dies, the other owner does *not* automatically get the deceased owner's share, which goes to the deceased owner's heirs. This type of ownership is more often seen when friends or siblings or business partners, rather than spouses, own an asset, such as a vacation cottage or business, together. When one owner dies, his share of the asset is a probate asset.

Finally, there are life estates, which divide the ownership of property, not so much among a number of current owners, but among a combination of current and future owners. The most common example is when an elderly person transfers the family home to his children, but reserves the right to live in the house for the remainder of his life. The children own the house, but cannot (legally) evict the parent from the house during the parent's lifetime. (Note: this kind of ownership can be extremely troublesome, and I would strongly advise anyone who's considering it to seek out professional advice from a local lawyer with estate planning experience before executing a deed containing a life estate.) When the person who owns the life estate (generally, the elderly parent) dies, the life estate is terminated, and there is nothing left for the probate court to manage. Accordingly, it is a non-probate asset.

Insurance policies and some annuities can be viewed as part of the general category of a life estate. The person whose life is insured owns the policy during his lifetime, but when he dies, the portion of the policy that he was entitled to is terminated, and the remainder is paid to a named beneficiary without going through the estate. Accordingly, life insurance policies and some annuities are non-probate assets (unless the named beneficiary is the estate). Note, however, that there may be some tax reporting required for the life insurance or annuity pay-out, even if the assets are not part of the probate assets.

Take a look at your inventory, and make a note whether each item is part of your probate assets or non-probate assets. Only your probate assets will be subject to the directions in your will.

Now that you know what your assets are, and whether they will be subject to the probate court's jurisdiction, you can start thinking about what will happen to your assets when you're no longer able to manage them.

Chapter 4: Who will be getting those assets?

There's an urban legend that if you don't have a will, the state will take all of your assets when you die. In most circumstances, that is simply not true.

If you don't have a will (or a comparable estate planning document), your state has laws that will determine who gets your assets, both real and personal, tangible and intangible. These laws are generally referred to as the laws of intestate succession or intestate distribution, with "intestate" simply referring to a person who dies without a will. These laws require a complete absence of any locateable heirs before the state will take your assets.

Nevertheless, you should have some idea of who your state thinks are your preferred beneficiaries, in case you disagree with the state's priorities. The details of who gets what varies somewhat from state to state.

The Uniform Probate Code sets out priorities that

are in keeping with the priorities of the majority of states, whether or not they adopted the specific language of the Uniform Code. The priorities, in a simplified form here, are: 1. If the deceased person had a surviving spouse, but no surviving parents or children, then the spouse takes the entire estate. 2. If the deceased person had a surviving spouse, plus either parents or children, the estate is divided between the spouse and the other surviving heirs (parents, children or both). 3. If the deceased person had no spouse, then his children share the entire estate. 4. If the deceased person had no spouse, children or parents, then the next closest kin share the estate.

Under the Uniform Probate Code, and in most, possibly all, other states, adopted children are treated the same as biological children. If you have an adopted child, however, you should double-check how your state handles this issue by consulting with a qualified legal professional.

Make a note of who your heirs are, according to your state's intestate succession laws, so you'll have an idea of what will happen if you don't have a will. Make sure to consider the worst- case scenarios. Just because you currently have a spouse or sibling or best friend who could make the most of the inheritance, you can't rest completely easy. What if that competent person dies before you? Who would be next in line to inherit? Is that person good with money and with sharing with other beneficiaries? Consider, too, whether any of your likely heirs are minors.

Do any of your heirs have issues, like mental illness or addiction, that would prevent them from managing an inheritance responsibly? Do you need to take steps so that incompetent, spendthrift, greedy or litigious heirs can benefit from the inheritance without dissipating it? (Perhaps now you can see why lawyers so often turn to storytelling; we're trained to anticipate worst-case scenarios, and in our fiction, we can play out those scenarios, with every possible complication.)

Once you have your list of heirs according to your state laws, it may appear at first glance that you can trust those laws to take care of your estate. It's entirely possible. Alternatively, you may simply not have the pessimistic thought processes of a trained estate planner, so you haven't begun to imagine all the things that can go wrong. Are you willing to take that risk? If so, then you can skip to the chapter on literary representatives. If not, then continue reading about the trouble that may ensue when relying on the laws of intestate succession.

While the states' probate laws are intended to match the "typical" person's wishes, they present a couple complications, even for a relatively simple estate. First, they frequently provide for the deceased person's minor children to inherit a share of the estate. In many situations, it would be better for the surviving spouse to have full control over the entire estate, especially when that spouse is also the parent of the minor children, at least during the surviving spouse's lifetime. Otherwise, the surviving spouse will have to file for a legal guardianship of the children, in order to manage their inheritance for them, will be limited in what the assets can be used for, and may have to account to the court for even the most routine expenditures. A cash inheritance in those circumstances isn't a huge hassle, but if the children inherit a partial interest in real estate, it can significantly complicate the sale or refinance of the asset, increasing legal fees and wasting time, even when the sale or refinancing is clearly in the children's best interests.

Second, on the other end of the age spectrum, the standard intestate priorities would have assets go to the parents of someone without a spouse or children, rather than to siblings or nieces or nephews. (Parents are closer kin than siblings.) Having assets go to an older generation (parents) instead of a younger generation (siblings or nieces/nephews) may not make any financial sense. Imagine what would happen if a sixty-something person died without a will, leaving behind no spouse or children, just his octogenarian parents, plus a bunch of thirty-something nieces and nephews. The assets would go through the sixty-something's estate to the octogenarian parents, who would likely die a short time later, without having used up the assets (unless the inheritance disqualifies them for Medicaid, and is spent on their nursing home expenses), so that the same assets will go through the costs associated with probate before eventually ending up with the nieces and nephews, minus the cost of probate and minus whatever was claimed by Medicaid.

Spend a few minutes thinking like a lawyer. Or like a novelist plotting out worst-case scenarios to throw at your characters. Take your state's intestacy rules, and apply them to the members of your family. Consider all the possible scenarios that might happen between now and the (many, many, many) years from now when your estate will be probated. Who will your heirs be then? How many of them, given their current circumstances, will still be alive? What if the otherwise unthinkable happens, and tragedy strikes the young and healthy ones? Who will they leave behind that you would like to benefit from your estate? If you have a particularly small family, which could too easily be wiped out, is there a charity that you would like to name as a last defense against your assets escheating to the state?

Chapter 5: Contested estates

A will contest is like the Spanish Inquisition: no one expects it. I doubt any parent expects his or her children to be fighting over pots and pans and dilapidated furniture, and yet it happens far too often.

If you think about it, though, you can see why the squabbles bubble up to the surface so frequently. For one thing, the loss of a loved one is automatically a stressful event, which clouds a person's judgment and unpacks all sorts of emotional baggage. It's not really the pots and pans that the heirs are fighting over; it's what those pots and pans symbolize about their relationships with the deceased person.

The naturally stressful situation is complicated further by family dynamics. Maybe the family members have been scattered all over the country, and aren't used to working as a unit. Maybe they've been living near each other all their lives, and the proximity has given rise to an accumulation of resentment that makes them hyper-sensitive to any perceived slights in a will or during the distribution of family mementoes.

Now, add in assets that are actually valuable, rather than the symbolic pots and pans, and the potential for friction grows exponentially. Even estates that seem, at first glance, to be managed cooperatively and peacefully, without any formal contests, are often mere facades, covering seething resentment and anxiety and doubts and misunderstandings. This kind of angst is fun to read about in fiction, but presumably you'd like to protect your heirs from experiencing it in real life.

There are three basic legal grounds for contesting a will: incompetence of the testator (the person who executed the will), technical defects in the will, or evidence that the will was executed involuntarily (fraud or duress).

A person who is legally incompetent cannot execute a will, and the issue of the testator's competence is a fertile source of will contests. Wills often start with a statement that the testator is "of sound and disposing mind and memory." It's such a standard bit of boilerplate that in most cases, neither the testator nor the attorney drafting the will actually gives this language much thought.

In most cases, there's no need to dwell on the testator's competence, but it can come up later, especially if the various heirs don't like the terms of the will. At that point, it's not always easy to tell, given the passage of time, whether the testator was competent at the time he signed the will. Obviously, if the testator was the subject of a guardianship when the will is executed, it may well be invalid. But what if a guardian was appointed a week after the signing? Would you infer that he was incompetent a week earlier? What if the guardian wasn't appointed until a month later? Six months later? Conversely, the lack of a legal guardian at the time of the signing is no guarantee that the testator was competent then. The testator could have been under the influence of narcotics or alcohol, or could have been in the early stages of dementia, drifting in and out of competence.

The next basis for a will contest is some defect in the technical requirements. The laws have relaxed many of these requirements, but some are needed to deal with the competence issue, and to minimize the chance of giving legal effect to a forged will. Most, if not all, states require that a will be witnessed by two people (who are not also beneficiaries under the will), plus a notary. The standard language for a witness clause generally recites that the witness saw the testator sign the will, and that the witness believes the testator to be of sound mind and memory. In addition, a typical notary clause for a will reiterates the witnesses' belief that the testator was of sound mind and memory.

While the notary may not specifically offer any judgment in the notary clause as to the testator's competence, the conclusion is implicit in the notary's signature. Each state has its own specific rules for notaries, but they are generally consistent with the guiding principles in the National Notaries Association's ethics rules. One of those principles is "The Notary shall require the presence of each signer and oath-taker in order to carefully screen each for identity and willingness, and to observe that each appears aware of the significance of the transaction requiring a notarial act." The commentary on that principle explains, "The Notary shall not notarize for any person if the Notary has a reasonable belief that can be articulated that the person at the moment is not aware of the significance of the transaction requiring a notarial act." This is essentially a requirement that the notary not notarize any document, including a will, signed by someone who is incompetent.

While the technical requirements for executing a will are intended to safeguard against fraudulent or otherwise unreliable wills, they can also be fertile grounds for will contests, usually when the will was written by the testator himself without the assistance of a legal professional. I have seen at least one will that was drafted from a form book, and treated by the testator as his will, with the clear intent that it be probated, even though he never bothered to actually sign it. More commonly, a testator will sign a typed will, thinking that it qualifies as a holographic will (there's an exception in some states to requiring witnesses, when the entire will is written in the testator's own handwriting), so he didn't bother with the necessary witnesses. I haven't experienced it myself, but there are reported cases of wills that were signed by a testator, and that even had witness signatures, but the heirs are able to prove that the testator was in one room, and the witnesses were another, so they didn't see the will signed or get an acknowledgment from the testator that he had signed it and wanted them to witness it. Such a will is invalid, because of the risk that the unseen testator did not, in fact, willingly sign the will.

Thus, the final ground for contesting a will is evidence that the testator did not sign it willingly. For fraud, the fact pattern is usually something along the lines of an allegation that the testator, with bad eyesight, was told he was simply signing a routine document, like a letter to his grandchildren, when he was actually signing a will. The technical requirements for witnesses and a notary are intended to minimize this kind of blatant fraud, so it isn't seen very often.

More common is the allegation that the testator was the victim of duress. It usually isn't the typical duress claim, that the person signed a document at gunpoint, but a kinder, gentler duress generally referred to as "undue influence." The notary clause is intended to minimize this problem. The commentary to the same ethics principle quoted above includes a prohibition on notarizing a document when the signer is under undue influence: "The Notary shall not notarize for any person if the Notary has a reasonable belief that can be articulated that the person is being bullied, threatened, intimidated or otherwise unduly influenced into acting against his or her will or interest."

Undue influence, however, is much more difficult for a notary to recognize. It's pretty obvious if a testator can't answer a question about his name and address. It's not so obvious whether a testator is legitimately grateful to someone in his will, or is being bullied by that person. The most common scenario for an allegation of undue influence is when an elderly parent leaves his entire estate (or a disproportionately large percentage of the estate) to only one of his several children, and that disproportionate beneficiary is the child who has been living with and caring for the elderly parent. It's always possible that the parent gave the caretaker child the entire estate in gratitude for what the caretaker gave up in his own life. It's equally possible that the parent was bullied by the caretaker into disinheriting the other children.

The bottom line is that you simply cannot, within the structure of the American legal system, absolutely prevent a determined troublemaker from contesting a will, but you can take steps to minimize the potential for such litigation. The first thing you can do is to execute a well-drafted will, preferably under the supervision of a legal profession who will make sure the technical requirements have been met.

The other thing you can do to minimize the risk of a will contest is to communicate your wishes to your family. You'll be giving your personal representative (and possibly the successor nominee) a copy of your will. Consider giving copies to all of your closest family members. Talk to them about the terms, so that they will be clear that the will is truly what you want, and not a matter of undue influence. If you will be making an unequal distribution, discuss your rationale with the heirs, so that they know why you chose to do so. If you can't talk to them, perhaps consider writing them a letter, explaining your decision. We are writers, after all, and can often write better than we can talk!

In some states, you can include an "in terrorem" clause in your will, which provides that any person contesting the will is prohibited from inheriting under the will. The Uniform Probate Code renders these clauses invalid, but individual states can choose, like Massachusetts did, not to adopt that particular section of the code, so that they still enforce these clauses. I wouldn't generally recommend relying too heavily on the clause, however, since there is a bit of a catch-22: if you contest the will and win, the will is no longer valid, so neither is the *in terrorem* clause. The clause might prevent the most frivolous of contests, but is unlikely to deter anyone who believes he has a really strong basis for contesting the will. Unfortunately, in my experience, an angry and hurt family member will be unable to distinguish between frivolous and legitimate grounds for a will contest, and will often reject solid legal advice in favor of hiring an attorney who will mirror back to the client exactly what the client wants to hear, and will pursue a will contest against all odds.

While no one wants his estate to be contested, it can be a particularly expensive problem for authors. Will contests take time, and when lawyers talk about delays, they don't mean a few days or weeks. They mean, at a minimum, several months, more likely stretching into years. You probably know how important timing can be in publishing. Now, imagine that you've got a publishing contract up for renewal or at the point where you might seek reversion of your rights, or there's a formatting glitch with a book selling through an online retailer, which needs to be fixed or the book will be pulled from sale. Your will would give someone authority to deal with it, but only if that will isn't tied up in a contest over whether the will is valid or who should be the personal representative. As long as your will is actively being contested, there may not be anyone with authority to act on your behalf, and your books may be in limbo, not generating any income, and not remaining in your readers' thoughts.

Chapter 6: Managing Copyrights

Overview of copyright

Now that you know the basics of the probate process and the issues that arise in all estate plans, it's time to talk about the biggest complication for an author's estate plans: copyrights.

A "copyright" is the right to make copies of a creative work. For an author (as opposed to a painter or sculptor), a copyright is essentially the right to print or make digital copies of your stories, or to authorize someone else (publisher or digital retailer) to print or make digital copies of your stories.

Copyright law is intended to balance the rights of the creative person (the author) with the rights of society in general. Authors need to be able to generate income from their writing, and society derives benefits from public access to art and the wide dissemination of ideas.

The compromise that current copyright law embodies has three elements. First, ideas, per se, separate from the specific expression of those ideas, cannot be copyrighted, so everyone is encouraged to share ideas as widely as possible. Second, authors are granted an exclusive right to control and profit from their *expression* of ideas (the specific wording of stories or essays or poems themselves) for a lengthy but still limited period. And third, at the end of the exclusivity period, the *expressions* (the specific words) join the underlying ideas in the public domain, where they can be used and copied by anyone. (Plagiarism is a separate issue; even if stories are in the public domain, they should be properly attributed when they are used or copied.)

For written works created on or after January 1, 1978, the copyright for anything written by an identifiable individual author (not a corporation or other business entity) extends for seventy years after the author's death (or the death of the last author, if there is more than one). The rules prior to that date are more complicated, and beyond the scope of this book, as are the rules addressing work-for-hire, when the copyright is held by a business entity, not an individual. If your works fall into one of those categories, you can find more information at the United States Copyright Office's website, http://www.copyright.gov, starting with their "copyright basics" PDF.

Note too that there are special rules for the duration of copyright for anonymous or pseudonymous works. If you have registered your copyright, identifying yourself as the author, then the duration is the same as if your real name were listed on the book. If you have not registered your copyright on a pseudonymous work, identifying yourself as the author, the duration of the copyright runs from the publication date, rather than your date of death.

Will your book last that long?

You may be thinking that, as a popular fiction author, your books are ephemeral and will be forgotten well before the copyright period is up. You're probably aware that one strategy for maintaining brisk sales of your backlist is simply to keep writing and publishing new books, which tend to generate interest in the backlist. It's possible that when you stop writing new books, your old books may languish and fall into obscurity.

On the other hand, some books are likely to have a significant life expectancy even without new releases. Romance author Jennifer Crusie believes "it's a huge mistake to think that only literary authors last, especially since so many of them don't. If you look at nineteenth century literature, you'll see it was the popular authors like Austen and Dickens who've lasted, not the more highly regarded literary lions. 'Literature' changes with the times; good storytelling is forever."

No one can predict which books will last and which won't. What if yours is one of the keepers and continues to generate income for the life of your copyright and beyond? You might as well make arrangements for that possibility. According to paranormal romance author Diane

Whiteside, the third of four generations of writers in her family, "I would have said seventy years is far too long to worry about ... except my grandfather's books are still for sale on Amazon fifteen years after his death!"

The problem of time and multiplication

As you can imagine, the lengthy duration of copyright can give rise to a variety of complications. For starters, your copyrights (and any contracts you may have signed to license your copyright to a publisher) will need to be managed for considerably longer than the standard two or three year timeframe of a probate proceeding.

Think about what it means for an asset to last for seventy years. That's an entire lifetime for one person. Enough time for several generations of heirs to be born and die.

Let's say you are fortunate enough to live, and to write prolifically, to your one hundred and first birthday. Let's assume further that you wish your copyrights to benefit your spouse and your descendants. If you and each subsequent generation reproduced at age 30 and your descendants inherited your long-lived genes, then when you turned 100, you would have children close to 70 years old, grandchildren close to 40 years old and great-grandchildren close to ten years old. Now, add seventy years (the duration of copyright) to those ages, to calculate how many heirs will exist before the copyright expires.

You'd have great-great grandchildren after twenty years, and great-great-great grandchildren at fifty years. If any of your heirs got a little bit ahead of the family pattern, procreating at age 20 instead of 30, you could even have great-great-great-great (four greats!) grandchildren before the copyrights expire. Presumably, some of those intervening generations lost a member or two to death, possibly leaving surviving spouses with interests in the deceased heir's share of the copyrights. Even if each generation only had two children, and all of the spouses' shares came back into the blood descendants' hands, there could be as many as 64 people in the last group of heirs, consisting of triple-great and quadruple-great grandchildren, all of whom had a share of the copyrights, and all of whom were entitled to a voice in the management of those copyrights. Copyrights can't generally be divided up neatly and permanently in a single distribution. It's a simple process to divide a bank account among however many heirs you have at the time of your death. The total balance in the account (after payment of expenses) can be divided by the number of heirs, and each one gets his or her share, to do with as he or she pleases from that moment on. Most other types of assets can be divided mathematically like a bank account (*e.g.*, stock certificates or bonds) or can be turned into cash that can be divided mathematically (*e.g.*, jewelry or art collections).

A copyright, however, cannot be broken up that

easily. Copyrights are comparable in some ways to real estate, which can be owned for long periods of time, and cannot easily be broken into physical pieces to share among the heirs (*e.g.*, the widow gets the second floor of the family home, and each of the two children gets half of the first floor, with everyone having an easement to use the hallways). Conflicts among joint owners of real estate, however, can be resolved by a well-defined legal procedure ("petition to partition") that forces the owners to sell the property, and then distribute the proceeds.

Much like a piece of real estate, a single copyright cannot be divided mathematically, assigning a certain number of words or pages or chapters to each heir, who can then publish each section on his own. Instead, the heirs will need to work together, potentially for seventy years, keeping the book(s) intact, finding the best publishing and distribution options, and then sharing the net profits. Unlike real estate, however, copyrights don't have the benefit of any clearly defined legal procedure to force a sale when the owners can't work together. The joint owners of copyrights are therefore left to their own devices, hammering out resolutions where possible, wasting the opportunities for generating income by failing to reach an agreement, or engaging in expensive piecemeal litigation to resolve their differences every time a new disagreement occurs.

Even if you have enough copyrighted books so that your personal representative could divide them evenly, giving each of your initial heirs the copyrights to specific books, it's only a temporary solution, and not a particularly satisfying one. Breaking up the management of the copyrights that way, with each heir doing something different with the book(s) under his control, could affect the branding, marketing, and overall sales. Plus, there's the difficulty of assessing the value of each book to be sure the distribution is fair. Some books may be more popular and sell better than others, so simply distributing an equal number of copyrights to each heir would not necessarily be an equal distribution. Finally, even if the number of copyrights could be divided equally among the initial set of heirs who are entitled to shares at the time of your death, the long duration of copyright makes it almost inevitable that the initial set of heirs will die before the copyright expires, so that the copyrights will need to be divided at least once more, possibly several times, among the spouses and children of the initial set of heirs, before the seventy years are up.

Once again, you inevitably run into problems that arise out of too many people with a right to participate in the management of your copyrights. What if one person wants to self-publish them, and another wants to license them to a publisher? What if one person wants to license them to Publisher A, and another wants to license them to Publisher B? As we've seen above, there could easily be sixty or more people with a different vision for your copyrights.

Factor in the additional chaos that could ensue from the fact that most, if not all, of those sixty heirs are unlikely to have any expertise whatsoever in the publishing industry. Try to think back to when you first started writing, and then started to learn about the publishing industry (including both trade publishing and self-publishing). Do you remember how insane you thought the standard industry practices were? How long did it take you to figure out what was, in fact, "normal" in the industry? How fast does "normal" change in the industry? How many mistakes did you make while trying to figure out how the industry works?

Many spouses support the author by offering a sympathetic ear, but aren't actively involved in the various publishing decisions an author must make. If your spouse (or other initial heir) is similarly situated, would your spouse be willing and able to step up and learn all about publishing, in order to manage your copyrights after you're gone? Alternatively, perhaps your spouse has, in fact, been helping you with your decisions about your copyrights, and can manage them after your death, guiding the rest of your heirs. But, as you're probably tired of hearing me say, you can't think just about who is likely to be alive on the day of your funeral. It's highly unlikely that your spouse probably won't be alive fifty years after your death. Do your other heirs (and their children, and unborn subsequent generations) know as much about publishing as your spouse does? Are they going to have the time and inclination to learn?

Keep in mind that, unless you take steps to change the default situation, *all* of your heirs will need to agree before any action can be taken with respect to your copyright. There's no law that says the majority rules in this kind of disagreement. Decisions with respect to your copyright must be unanimous or taken to court.

Have you ever tried to get twenty or thirty or sixty people to agree on *anything*? Even something as simple as when and where to hold a meeting to agree on substantive matters? What do you think the chances are that twenty or more of your heirs could reach an anonymous decision, when the choices are subjective, and the results will significantly increase or lower their income? Now, factor in the likelihood that some of your heirs know nothing about publishing. All it takes is one of your heirs to be ignorant of the publishing industry, and therefore have unrealistic expectations or plans, and that one heir could bring the whole enterprise to a halt.

You may be thinking that a simple answer is to let the personal representative (or successor representative) of your estate manage the copyrights for their full duration, paying the net proceeds to the appropriate heirs. The problem is that the personal representative will have authority over the copyrights only as long as the probate proceeding is ongoing. At some point, however, generally within three years of the date of death, the personal representative will be expected to distribute the estate's assets, including the literary ones, to the heirs. After the distribution, the estate will be closed out, and neither the personal representative nor the probate court will have any authority to manage or control the copyrights. Instead, the heirs will need to manage the copyrights, or take the matter to the appropriate civil trial court for resolution.

There is a simple solution, in the form of a literary representative (see chapter 7 below), but it won't happen unless you have a will or comparable estate planning document.

The problem of the right to rescind a prior transfer of copyright

There is one additional problem for authors, which can arise out of an odd little provision copyright law with respect to transfers of copyrights during the author's lifetime.

Copyrights may be transferred or assigned, in whole or in part, during the author's lifetime, as part of the probate process or after distribution from the estate. During your lifetime, you can assign a certain portion of your rights a publisher or digital distributor. These contracts are best thought of as a license, rather than a transfer. The publisher doesn't "own" the copyright, but is simply renting the right to print and distribute the work, subject to certain terms. In contrast, work-for-hire contracts are transfers of the entire copyright from the author to the entity contracting for the work.

Some publishers of the less-than-savory variety may attempt to acquire the entire copyright of an author, in non-work-for-hire situations. In such cases, federal copyright law provides a remedy to safeguard authors "against unremunerative transfers. A provision of this sort is needed because of the unequal bargaining position of authors, resulting in part from the impossibility of determining a work's value until it has been exploited."

The safeguard consists of the right to rescind the transfer during a five-year window, beginning either "thirty-five years from the date of publication of the work under the grant or at the end of forty years from the date of execution of the grant, whichever term ends earlier." 17 U.S.C. 203(a)(3). In other words, if you had assigned your entire copyright to a sleazy publisher on January 1, 2000, and came to regret it, you would have the right, between January 1, 2035 and January 1, 2040, to terminate the publisher's ownership of your copyright. (It may be cold comfort, having to wait that many years, but it's better than nothing.)

While this statute is well-meaning, it addresses only one situation where a copyright has been assigned in its entirety. There is another situation, where an author makes a gift of one or more of the copyrights to friends or family, during the author's lifetime. I expect to see more and more authors doing just that. Historically, such transfers weren't particularly feasible, due to the various challenges of dealing with a trade publisher. In the past, most authors (other than a very few at the top) have had a small number of copyrights actually generating money, with most of the backlist languishing out of print. Today, backlists are generating income, which increases the number of active copyrights that an author can parcel out. In addition, self-published authors tend to be more prolific than trade-published authors were in the past, which also increases the number of active copyrights an author has. The more income-producing copyrights an author has, the greater the opportunity to make a gift of one or more of those copyrights. As explained below, in Chapter 11, giving away assets during your lifetime can be a useful estate planning tool. The very nature of self-publishing, which cuts out the various middlemen, makes it easier for an author today to make a gift of copyright, by publishing a book and then immediately transferring the copyright to a beneficiary who will receive all of the profits.

The federal copyright law, however, did not anticipate the potential for voluntary and intentional transfers of whole copyrights during the author's lifetime. (Note that the right of rescission does not apply to transfers made by will, so this issue only arises when you've made a transfer during your lifetime.) Let's say that you have a friend or family member who has a special connection with one of your books, and you would like to give that person the entire copyright to that particular book. Maybe you wrote it to benefit a charity, and would like to simply give the copyright to the charity, to manage as it sees fit. You certainly have the legal authority to do just that, either during your lifetime or in your will. If you do it during your lifetime, however, it will be subject to the right to terminate the transfer.

Obviously, if you make an intentional gift of the copyright, you aren't likely to turn around and terminate the transfer. But what if you died before the termination period began? The law does not allow you to specify in your will, or in any other document, who can terminate the transfer of copyright. In simplest terms, only the surviving spouse and children (or, if neither exist, then the grandchildren) can rescind the gift. In many situations, your spouse and/or children may be the appropriate persons to decide whether to terminate a transferred copyright. In other situations, however, they are exactly the wrong persons for that decision.

Consider, for example, a married author, knowing that he is terminally ill, who decides to give his mistress the copyright on one of his more popular books, to provide for her, without having to name her in his will, which would embarrass both the wife and the mistress. The author then dies, the widow finds out about the transfer of the copyright to the mistress, and, on the first day of the rescission period, revokes the transfer. The mistress, who was clearly the author's intended beneficiary, would no longer own the copyright, and the widow (or her heirs) would have the copyright instead.

Perhaps you're not sympathetic to the mistress, but consider a variation on the same theme: the married, dying author has children by a prior marriage. He makes a gift of approximately half of his copyrights to his beloved children during his lifetime, and leaves the rest, in his will, to his current wife and her children (the author's stepchildren). This time, the widow is a scheming hussy who always hated the author's children, so she too is waiting eagerly for the first day of the rescission period, so she can revoke the transfer at the first opportunity. The author's children are robbed of their inheritance, while the greedy widow and stepchildren claim the whole estate.

Yet another complication might arise if you initially register your copyright under your name individually and later transfer the copyright to a trust or business entity (*e.g.*, LLC or corporation). I have not seen any cases on the subject, but the statute itself makes no distinction between transfers to unrelated third parties (*i.e.*, a publisher) and transfers to an entity that the author owns (LLC or corporation created by the author). It is not at all clear, from a legal point of view, what would happen if you transferred your copyrights to an LLC or trust as part of an estate plan, and then your heirs decided they didn't like the restrictions you may have written into that LLC or trust, so they get together and revoke the transfers into the LLC or trust, so that they will then own the copyrights without restrictions, and without all the safeguards you tried to impose to protect your heirs from a stupid course of action like this would be.

Once again, there is a simple solution if you are aware of the potential problem and deal with it in your will. If you make a gift of a copyright during your lifetime, you should also make a specific bequest of that copyright to the same person (or trust or business entity) in your will. Then, if the assignment of the copyright were to be revoked, the copyright would return to your estate, to then be distributed back to the person you originally gave it to. In other words, by making the gift again in your will, even though it seems redundant, you've taken away the incentive for anyone to revoke the original gift of the copyright.

Chapter 7: Literary Representatives

What is a literary representative?

A literary representative isn't well defined in the law. It's probably best to think of the literary representative as a trustee, charged with managing the trust assets (the literary assets) on behalf of the beneficiaries (the heirs entitled to a share of the copyrights' profits). It's also similar to a limited power of attorney, whereby one person (a "grantor") gives another person (the "attorney," who does not have to be a lawyer) the power to do things the grantor could have done himself with respect to certain assets, *i.e.*, the deceased person's assets.

A literary representative essentially takes your place in all decisions relating to your copyrights, following whatever instructions you may have provided in the document that appoints the literary representative. The literary representative can be a literary agent, directly negotiating deals on behalf of your heirs, but doesn't have to be. The literary representative can simply be one of your heirs, who is stepping into your shoes, choosing the agent and then discussing and making the final decisions with respect to the various offers the agent may be able to elicit.

Why do you want a literary representative?

If you're a business-oriented author, you probably don't need a lot of convincing about the importance of appointing a literary representative. As paranormal romance author Diane Whiteside says, "My works are a money-making asset. All money-making assets should have a designated person who will oversee them after my death. Period. I wouldn't dream of not having a literary executor, any more than I'd not have an executor for my other assets."

You may not be that business-focused, though, and you're skeptical. Lots of authors die without appointing a literary agent, after all, so you may be wondering what the big deal is. It's true that lots of authors don't have literary representatives (or any will at all), but that doesn't make it a good decision. In most cases, it reflects procrastination, rather than a conscious decision. They simply haven't thought about the consequences of their death, or the various complications outlined in the previous chapter. It's not unlike the number of parents of young children who don't have wills. If they thought about it, they would probably be appalled to realize that someone they consider to be a horrible parent might well be the court's first choice for guardianship of their children.

You don't have the excuse of ignorance. You've read about the dozens of heirs who may have a say in the management of your copyrights, the need for unanimity, and the problem of heirs who don't understand publishing norms. Wouldn't it make more sense to have just one person who can make all those decisions? Someone who will either have publishing industry knowledge or who, by virtue of being responsible for so many people's wellbeing, will have an incentive to learn about the publishing industry?

Non-fiction author Virginia McCullough realized she needed a literary representative when her children were young. She explained, "I wanted to be certain that if something were to happen to me, my children would receive the royalties." McCullough also considers the volatility of the publishing industry as an additional reason for needing a literary representative, and this is certainly true now, more than ever. The volatility means that even a book that's under contract and selling well still need some supervision. She gave the example of one of her early books, which remained in print through several editions and with a couple different publishers as a result of multiple sales/mergers of the original publisher. Self-publishers know just how much work it is to oversee the sales and marketing of their backlists.

Naming a literary representative won't solve all of the problems that arise out of ownership of copyrights. Obviously, the person you choose isn't likely to survive the full seventy years of the copyright, but you can establish a procedure for choosing the successor, so that there will only be one voice speaking for you.

What qualities should a literary representative have?

So, how do you choose a literary representative? The only mandatory requirement is that the literary representative needs to be a competent adult. In other words, the literary representative needs to be at least the age of majority for your state and mentally competent at the time you nominate them, and remain competent for the duration of their appointment.

The representative can be either a professional (*e.g.*, a literary agency or law firm) or non-professional (*e.g.*, a family member). A professional may be the better choice where the author has several bestselling books in print, complicated contracts across various media and in several countries, or a multitude of heirs with divergent ideas about how to manage the copyrights. Choosing a professional representative also has the advantage of longevity; an established literary agency or law firm is likely to survive longer than any individual person.

Some authors, like paranormal romance author Diane Whiteside, are fortunate enough to have several family members with publishing expertise, so they have several options for choosing a literary representative. In most cases, however, if you choose a literary representative from among your relatives, it would be someone who has never been directly involved in the publishing industry.

Make sure you think about the choice of literary representative carefully. Your spouse (or sibling or adult child) might be a great choice to be your personal representative, managing your real estate, cars and cash, especially with the assistance of a legal or financial professional that you chose during your lifetime. At the same time, your spouse (or other family member) may not be the right person to manage your literary assets, even with the assistance of your agent or other professionals you worked with during your lifetime.

If you're trade published, would your chosen family member be capable of negotiating a contract, terminating a contract or getting rights reverted? Would that person understand the pros and cons of these actions, even if there was an agent doing the actual negotiation, termination and reversion? Keep in mind that an agent (who is not also the literary representative) can advise, but can't make final decisions about the copyright; only the owner of the copyright (the literary representative) can make the decisions. If you're self-published, would your literary representative be capable of finishing any incomplete manuscripts or finding someone who could, releasing any completed but not yet published works, and marketing these new books along with the backlist?

At a minimum, your literary representative should be familiar with publishing terminology, how advances and royalties work, the differences and similarities between trade and self-publishing, the duration of copyright, and the differences (in sales and content) among genres. Keep in mind that unless you live in New York City, it is unlikely that any professional (agent, lawyer or other consultant) within a hundred miles of your home has the expertise to advise your literary representative on publishing issues, the way a financial advisor might be able to help your personal representative with management of other types of assets.

Another important trait for the literary representative is the ability to withstand pressure. Especially if there are several heirs sharing ownership of the copyrights, each with a different opinion about how the literary assets should be handled, the representative may come under significant pressure while making decisions. If the heirs come from a mixed family (first and second marriages), the pressures may be particularly intense.

It would seem unnecessary to mention that a literary representative, as a fiduciary (from the Latin word, *fides*, meaning "faith"), should be trustworthy, but the courts are filled with evidence of how elusive this trait can be. A famous literary example is Ernest Hemingway's estate. He reportedly made it widely known during his lifetime that he wished all of his unfinished manuscripts destroyed, but his literary representative ignored those wishes, and the works were published.

Collaborators may have special concerns when

choosing a representative, since the representative will need to work with both the writing partner and the publisher or digital retailer. If you write both collaborations and solo books, or if you write in multiple genres that are vastly different from each other (*e.g.*, fiction and non-fiction, or erotica and inspirational), you may wish to appoint two different literary representatives, one for each group of copyrights.

Empowering the representative

The personal representative of an estate has, as a matter of law, certain powers and duties. A literary representative, however, does not exist as a matter of law, but only has the powers and duties that are listed in the will or trust that appoints the literary representative.

The most common powers given to a literary representative include the power to make decisions with respect to the publication, sale, license or other exploitation of the copyright; the power to make decisions with respect to the completion or destruction of unfinished work; the power to terminate copyright licenses; and the right to sue for copyright infringement (a growing problem in the digital age).

The representative's compensation should also be addressed in the estate planning documents. If the representative is a literary agent or attorney, the representative will expect compensation at his or her usual rate, and the failure to provide for such compensation might result in the professional declining the appointment. If the representative is a family member, the failure to specify the amount of compensation (or lack thereof) may give rise to litigation, which is not in anyone's best interest.

Any other powers that the author wishes to grant to her representative may be specifically listed in the will or trust. For instance, if you're willing to have unfinished manuscripts published, you may grant your representative the authority to finish the manuscript or hire someone to do the work.

In some cases, it may be appropriate to restrict the representative's powers, when an issue can be anticipated and addressed directly in the will or trust, thereby bypassing the representative. For example, some authors, like Hemingway, prefer that unfinished manuscripts should be destroyed, and if so, that should be specified in the will itself, rather than leaving it to the discretion of the representative. For an author's early, unpublished works that may not live up to the standard of the later works or might otherwise tarnish the author's reputation, it may be wise to take even stronger pre-emptive measures now. As romance author Jennifer Crusie said, "Anything we really don't want published, we destroy."

Another potential source of conflict among heirs stems from possession of the physical manuscripts. (Note that possession of the manuscript does not, by itself, carry with it the right to publish the manuscript.) To minimize the chance of litigation over who should receive the author's papers, the will or trust can specify the person, university or museum who will receive them, essentially bypassing the discretion of the literary representative. The practice of donating papers for future study appears to be approaching extinction, however, as hand-written manuscripts are replaced with computer files. You may still have physical items of interest to scholars. Author Jenny Crusie makes collages that help her to understand her stories as she's writing or rewriting them. If you do something similar, or you keep your drafts or outlines, you could provide in your will for them to go to the educational or charitable institution of your choice.

Finally, a follow-up choice of representative should also be named, in case the first person is unable to accept the appointment or, after serving as representative, becomes unable to continue. Naming a succeeding representative isn't likely to be enough to cover the full lifetime of your copyright, so you should also provide instructions for how a subsequent representative would be chosen.

Guidance for your literary representative.

You can give your literary representative *carte blanche*, and trust his or her judgment completely. You'll probably feel comfortable giving this sort of authority to someone you know personally. But what about the person who will be acting in your behalf fifty years from your death, who may not even have been born before you died? Offering a few specific instructions may give both you and your literary representative some peace of mind.

One of the issues that come up frequently in writers' discussions of their work is what they want to happen with their unfinished manuscripts. Would you rather have all your unfinished manuscripts burned, or would you be comfortable with the prospect of someone else finishing them? Would you feel differently if the manuscript was in the proverbial "shitty first draft" as opposed to a second or third draft that's been out to beta readers and just needs a little polishing? What about all the false starts and outlines you have on your hard drive?

Romance author Jennifer Crusie realized she needed to do something when she noticed "dead authors continu[ing] to publish. As someone once said about a big author who'd died but whose books kept coming out, 'Death is no bar to publishing these days.'" Crusie was concerned about protecting not just her assets but also her reputation: "I don't want to see my name sold out."

If you have a particular literary reputation that you'd like to maintain, that should be explained in your instructions. As one judge wrote, while resolving a dispute among an authors' heirs, the "management of literary property is more than the economic stewardship of a ...

monopoly conferred upon an author under the copyright laws. How such literary property is exploited affects not only economic aspects of the author's works, but the esteem in which the author is held." *In the Matter of the Estate of Lillian Hellman*, 511 N.Y.S.2d 485 (1987).

The judge raises yet another reason to appoint a literary representative, separate from the personal representative for the estate. The estate's representative is a "traditional fiduciary," with a duty to emphasize "prosperity rather than posterity [and] may be forced to concern themselves solely with keeping the books rather than keeping the flame." *Id.* A literary representative may choose to turn down income, if the proposed use of the copyrights would damage the author's reputation.

If you wish, you can indicate if you have any preferences with respect to short-term versus long-term goals, *e.g.*, whether decisions should be primarily for the benefit of the current heirs, or if the literary representative should have a longer view, caring equally for future income and future heirs. In other words, if your literary representative were offered a publishing deal that would provide the current heirs with a big chunk of money, in return for granting of extensive rights that limited future income, would you want the literary representative to be able to accept the deal?

Finally, consider how much you care about the detailed instructions you leave for your literary representative. If you're providing them simply to assist your literary representative, but you won't be rolling over in your grave if they're not carried out, then the simplest way of handling them is to leave a memorandum, or letter, for your first choice of literary representative, with instructions to pass them along to successors. Under the Uniform Probate Code, the instructions in a memorandum are potentially enforceable in court, but you should not rely on that. First, your state may not have adopted the UPC, and in those states, a memorandum may not be enforceable. Second, even if your state has adopted the UPC, there is not much court interpretation of this clause of the statute, and I wouldn't be surprised if it is interpreted narrowly, simply to prevent frivolous claims based on purported memorandums. Accordingly, if the instructions you have for the literary representative are important enough that you want your heirs to be able to sue the literary representative for not following them to the letter, you should include them in your will.

You'll need to be reasonable in your expectations, however. You can't control absolutely everything (no matter how much some of us would like to), but you can at least give some guidance, both to make your literary representative's job easier, and to increase the odds that your wishes will be carried out.

What will your literary legacy be?

Your estate planning documents will be most successful if you know what you want your literary legacy to be, so you can explain your wishes to both your representative and the estate planning attorney. Think about what matters to you over both the short term and the long term, decide who you trust to carry out your wishes and then make an appointment with an estate planning attorney.

It's your literary legacy, after all, and you want to be sure your wishes are carried out with a minimum of expense and litigation, so no future judge will say about you, as was said of Lillian Hellman: "While her literary works can be characterized as creative genius, her will cannot."

Chapter 8: Death and taxes

If your estate is large enough, your personal representative may need to file an estate tax return, for either your state or the federal government. The details of estate taxes are beyond the scope of this book, so if you are concerned about them, you should discuss it with a local tax professional. If you'd like to read more about the federal estate tax, you can get an overview from the instructions for Form 706 at http://www.irs.gov.

For all the hype and fear about death taxes, very few authors are likely to pay any. (Note that, generally speaking, estate taxes are paid out of the estate, before the heirs receive the net assets. The heirs do not pay a federal tax on the assets they receive, only on interest or other income, like profits or royalties from your copyrights, that may accrue after the asset is transferred into the heirs' names.)

At present, an estate with less than five million dollars in probate assets will not even have to file a federal estate tax return, let alone owe any federal estate tax. Many states have the same threshold for filing, although some have a lower threshold, so this is also something to check with a local tax or estate planning professional.

There is one estate tax issue you should be aware of: the difficulty of placing a value on literary assets. A book contract with a trade publisher is somewhat easier to value, since there are some known dollar amounts: the balance of any advance due, with some adjustment for future royalties if you have a history of receiving royalties in addition to the advance. The value of a self-published book or the copyright on a manuscript that has not yet been published will be much more difficult to establish. Accordingly, if you think you'll have assets valued anywhere near the estate tax filing threshold for your state, it is particularly important for you to consult an estate planner. (See Chapter 9 below for more on getting the most out of meeting with professionals.) Trying to do your own estate plan when you have assets totaling five million dollars or more is the epitome of being penny wise and pound foolish.

Another tax that affects estate planning is the federal gift tax (and, depending on your state, possibly a state gift tax). Since an estate that has five million dollars in assets may be subject to an estate tax, you might think that one way to avoid that tax is to give away assets during your lifetime, to stay under the five million dollar threshold. Making gifts is, in fact, a common tool recommended by estate planners, but it has its limitations (and can give rise to the issue with the right to revoke those gifts, as explained above in Chapter 6).

Under current law, you can give away thirteen

thousand dollars per person, per year, without having to file a gift tax return. (Note that this limit doesn't apply to gifts to charities, which are not considered a "gift" for taxing purposes, but have other restrictions with respect to deductibility.)

In its simplest terms, the limitation on tax-free gifts means that if you have two children, you could give each of them thirteen thousand dollars without any tax consequences. (If your spouse joins you in making the gift, it can be twice as much.) If you have six grandchildren, you could give each of them thirteen thousand dollars without any tax consequences. You could make these thirteen thousand dollar gifts every year, if you wish. But if you, individually, give any more than thirteen thousand dollars to any one person in any one year, then you need to file a gift tax return.

You may be wondering what the gift tax rate is. This is where it gets a bit technical, because there isn't a gift tax rate. Instead, what happens is that the amount of the gift that exceeds thirteen thousand dollars is subtracted from the five million dollar threshold for an estate tax return. In other words, if you made two gifts to your child, one for the initial amount of thirteen thousand dollars, and then another for a million dollars, in order to reduce the size of your estate, you would need to file a gift tax return to report the million dollar gift. You wouldn't pay any tax then, but when it came time to calculate whether you needed to file (and pay) an estate tax, your threshold would be reduced from the standard five million by the million that you gave away. Your threshold would then be four million dollars, and, in essence, you would be paying a gift tax by paying an estate tax on the million dollars you gave away.

The reason this matters to authors, even if you don't have a five million dollar estate, is that you could inadvertently trigger the need to file a gift tax return by making a gift of your copyright on a particular book or series. You may wish to give one of your books, or a series of books, to a particular friend or family member during your lifetime, so that the recipient can collect the profits and manage the copyright in the future. Agatha Christie did this with some of her works, giving them to a nephew. Making a gift of a copyright isn't as simple as giving cash or stock certificates, because of the valuation problem: what is its fair market value on the day you make the gift? More or less than thirteen thousand dollars? What if you give away a book that turns out to be your breakout work, and you expected it to generate around ten thousand dollars, and it generates that much in the first month on the market? While you may be willing to take that risk, I strongly recommend that you consult with a local tax profession or lawyer before giving someone (other than a charity) the copyright on a book or series. This is an area where the risks of do-it-yourself can vastly overshadow the benefits.

Chapter 9: Making the Most of a Legal Consultation

Everyone needs a little help sometimes

Any document, like a will or trust appointing a literary representative, which may be in effect for as many as seventy years, has to be both flexible enough to address evolving family interests and publishing developments, while also being ironclad with respect to withstanding challenges to its validity. This is emphatically not the sort of document that you should do yourself, without professional guidance.

The choice of a lawyer to draw up these documents will have a long-lasting impact on your literary legacy, and therefore should be made as carefully as the choice of literary representative, using many of the same criteria. Ideally, the lawyer's expertise should encompass both estate planning law and the publishing industry. In most parts of the country, however, this will not be feasible, since publishing law is a micro-specialty seldom seen outside New York City. You may have to educate the lawyer on publishing issues and advise the lawyer about any specific powers you would like the literary representative to have (or not have), while leaving it up to the lawyer to make sure the technical requirements for the will are met.

Hiring someone to draft your will may go against your do-it-yourself inclinations, but it's in your best interest to resist the urge to practice law without a license. You can still retain considerable control, and minimize the cost of professional advice, by first educating yourself on the legal issues and then preparing for the appointment. Time is money, especially when consulting a professional whose charges are calculated at least in part by the amount of time spent on the case. Preparation can reduce the amount of time the professional will have to spend, while also maximizing the value of the document and advice you obtain.

Finding a lawyer

Field of expertise. Most lawyers, like doctors, have specialties. Depending on the state's rules, there may not be official specialties, like board-certified doctors, but most lawyers today generally limit their practices to no more than a few related categories. For contract review, you would want an attorney who specializes in publishing contracts, and for a royalty audit, you would want a certified public account who had experience with publishing contracts.

Most lawyers are capable of drafting a basic will and getting all the technicalities right, like the attestation clause and the appropriate number of witnesses. A will or trust that appoints a literary representative is unusual enough, however, that I would recommend that you find a lawyer who has some experience with actually probating wills, not just drafting them. A lawyer who only drafts wills, but has never had to usher one through the probate court is unlikely to be aware of all the pitfalls in a poorly drafted will. If you have a potentially taxable estate (*e.g.*, assets worth more than five million dollars at the federal level) or other complicated issues, beyond those involved with the management of copyrights (*e.g.*, heirs with mental disabilities or other special needs), you should upgrade to an attorney who specializes in estate planning.

Assuming your estate is otherwise straightforward, and you are working with a local probate lawyer, you should be prepared to educate the lawyer about the unique circumstances of an author's estate. When I first started thinking about appointing my own literary representative, I was familiar with the basics of wills from law school, and I'd been in a private practice for several years, where I'd drafted a few hundred wills for clients in assorted professions. I had never seen or read about anything comparable to a literary representative. Even when I did some basic legal research, looking for some sample language (lawyers generally prefer to work with language that's been proven to work, rather than starting from scratch in drafting a document), I came up with nothing. Obviously, attorneys have been drafting such provisions, but they just haven't made it into any of the usual resources. You can bring your attorney a copy of the samples in the appendices here, or refer them to *Lindey on Entertainment, Publishing and the Arts* (available in major law libraries and through Westlaw, using the abbreviation, LINDEY 3D).

The lawyer you hire for your will may run up against the same lack of information that I experienced. That doesn't mean you need to go to New York City and find a lawyer there who specializes in estate planning for authors. It just means you need to find a lawyer who's willing to be educated, and you need to be prepared to do the educating.

Get referrals and check them out. If you know anyone who's hired an attorney to probate the estate of a family member, ask for a referral. Funeral home directors, tax professionals, financial planners and insurance agents may also be good sources of referrals, especially for the more specialized estate planning lawyers.

If you can't get a referral to a probate attorney, see if you can get referrals to divorce lawyers. They often engage in what's known as a "family law" practice, which encompasses divorce, guardianship and probate.

Once you have several names to consider, research

them to see if there are any red flags that suggest you might not work well with any of them. Your state's bar association or regulatory board may have a website, where you can check to make sure the lawyer is, in fact, licensed in your state, and to see if there has been any history of disciplinary action. A quick check of the local phone book can often give you an idea of what size firm the professional is in, if that's something you care about, and what types of work the professional is interested in. Sometimes, the ads will indicate how long the professional has been licensed. More extensive information can be found in Martindale-Hubbell, available in some law libraries and courthouses, but unless you are an author on the scale of Stephen King or have a multi-million dollar estate in addition to the value of your copyrights, Martindale-Hubbell probably won't be as useful to you as simply talking to the local professionals you're considering.

Preparing for the appointment

The next step is to make a consultation appointment. You can maximize the time spent at the lawyer's office if you are prepared with a list of the names and addresses of all of your family members, the proposed literary representative (and successor), the proposed personal representative (and successor), and other beneficiaries outside your family, if any. A worksheet to collect this information is available for printing from my blog, http://www.thewritegin.blogspot.com

If you do not expect to work with the lawyer on anything other than the drafting of your will, it may not matter whether your personality meshes with the lawyer's. If you anticipate working with the lawyer on other aspects of your writing career, you may be more finicky about the choice of a lawyer. In that case, in addition to discussing what you want to accomplish with your will, you may wish to discuss the lawyer's expertise in that field of law, to find out if it's something the lawyer would be willing and able to handle. Even more important than that, you should be forming an impression of how well your personality meshes with the lawyer's.

What if you meet the professional, don't get any straight answers, or just get a bad vibe? Maybe you feel pressured to do a complicated estate plan, when all you want is something simple and straightforward. This scenario is why it's important to be prepared to say, "Thank you for your time" and leave without committing to anything further. There's no point in wasting your time or the professional's if the fit isn't right.

Pay attention to your gut reaction. If you dislike the professional on sight, then unless he's the only one within a five hundred mile radius, there's no reason to grit your teeth and work with him, no matter how extravagant the praise in referrals or how good the resume looked on paper. Thank the attorney for the consultation, leave without making any commitment, and resume the search for the right attorney for you.

Conversely, do *not* rely on a positive gut reaction as the sole reason for retaining a professional. Successful attorneys are salespeople, and it's their job to use their sales skills to charm you. Look past the facade, just as you look past the swanky (or not-so-swanky) office space. Make them show you their substantive skills.

Here are some things to consider: Do they listen to you, or do they ignore your input to focus on what they want to talk about? Are they willing to admit when they don't have an immediate answer? (Chances are, they've never represented a published author before, and there are many aspects of the bookselling industry that run counter to other industries, so cut them a little slack on extremely industry-specific matters.) If they don't have an immediate answer, are they willing to do some research and call you with an answer within a reasonable timeframe, probably a week or so? If they promise to call, do they follow through? The number one complaint to lawyers' governing boards is usually some variation on the fact that the lawyer failed to return calls in a timely manner. If the one you consult does that right from the beginning, it doesn't bode well for the future.

The goal is to find someone who not only has solid expertise, but is also someone you feel comfortable with.

Otherwise, move on to a second, third, however-many-you-need referral. The future of your copyrights is too important to place in the hands of someone you don't completely trust.

On the other hand, if you're uncomfortable with the first attorney you meet, make sure you're not simply blaming a perfectly good messenger for an answer you don't like. If, for example, the professional tells you that wills in your state require two witnesses plus a notary, all of them present in the room, watching you sign the will, and you're annoyed by prospect of performing in front of a crowd, but you'd liked the professional up until then, don't reject the professional simply for giving you valid but unwanted news. In other words, don't go looking for a professional who will only tell you what you want to hear. That kind of client-pleasing attorney, like a scam agent who promises you a spot on the bestseller lists if you'll just work with this particular kickback-paying book doctor, is worse than no attorney at all.

Chapter 10. Terms of your will

What the attorney needs to know.

As noted previously, unless you live in New York City, the chances are that your local attorney, who is professionally familiar with your state's requirements for a valid will, is not equally familiar with the special estate-planning concerns of an author. In fact, it's likely that you will be the only client the lawyer has ever represented who owns intellectual property that will need active management. If both you and the attorney feel comfortable working together, you can collaborate on your estate planning documents.

Some attorneys meeting with a client to draft estate planning documents will collect a detailed inventory of your assets, and others may only ask for a general overview. Very few will think to ask about whether you own any copyrights, and even if they ask, simply because it's on a checklist they copied from some continuing education program, they may not know exactly what to do when a client actually says yes to that question.

Normally, I recommend that clients seeking legal advice be prepared to present their *problem* to the attorney, not the *solution*. Too often, the proposed solution isn't the right one, and backtracking to figure out the actual problem can waste everyone's time. When creating a document that appoints a literary representative, though, I would recommend that you give the attorney the basic solution ("I need to appoint a literary representative"), along with the problem ("I own several copyrights that will outlast me and the probate process"), and then let the attorney figure out the best way to do that, given your state's laws and your unique circumstances.

The attorney doesn't need to know what, exactly, managing the copyrights entails; you just need to get the appointment of the literary representative written into the terms of the appropriate documents, along with any specific instructions you may have for the literary representative. Be prepared with the name and address of your proposed literary representative, and if you have a backup choice, provide that name and address. (You have checked with your nominees to make sure they're willing to take on the responsibility, right?)

If your first and second choices for your literary representative are current family members, such as a spouse or an adult child, you should also propose a method for choosing a literary representative when those choices are no longer willing or able to do the job. There are a number of options here, limited only by your imagination. If you can describe your preferences, the attorney can write them into the will.

One option is to allow each acting literary representative to name his or her successor, either before resigning or in his or her will. If you do that, you should have yet another backup plan, in case the literary representative dies unexpectedly without a will. One such option calls for something similar to a shareholder's meeting, during which all of your heirs who are entitled to a share of the royalties would vote on the replacement literary representative. If you go this route, I would advise against requiring anything more than a simple majority for electing a new literary representative, so as to avoid the paralysis that usually results from requiring unanimity. (I know, I know; your family would be able to get along for the common good. That's what everyone thinks, and it's too late to change the rules when it turns out that there's one bad apple among the heirs.)

Finally, you could nominate a professional trustee by referring to the financial institution with which the professional is affiliated. Financial institutions, and their trust departments, tend to endure, longer than individual human beings. A similar option, if you have a long-standing relationship with a literary agency, is to provide for the agency to take over the role of literary representative, in addition to the agenting duties, when your immediate family members are no longer able to fill the role. You need to make sure the literary agency is willing to take on the responsibility before naming it in your will. (Sorry, but you can't guarantee agency representation simply by dying. You have to suffer along with the rest of us, living through the query submissions and rounds of rejections, if you want a literary agent.)

You should also be prepared to tell the attorney if you want to impose any limits on the literary representative's authority, or offer any guidance to the literary representative for managing your copyrights. For instance, if you want all of your incomplete manuscripts burned, then say so. Or if you want incomplete manuscripts completed by a ghostwriter, then you can include that recommendation, with or without suggestions for finding a ghostwriter or specifying an ideal person to do the work. For instance, fantasy author Terry Pratchett has reportedly given his daughter the authority to finish his future works or to write in his fictional world.

Some other issues to mention in your will if you have strong feelings about them include: whether to authorize screenplays or stage plays based on your stories or characters, whether to authorize non-literary products based on your stories or characters, and how to address fanfiction. If you don't have strong feelings on these issues, you can simply not mention them, but particularly where you wish to limit the literary representative's authority (as opposed to leaving matters to the literary representative's discretion), you need to tell your attorney and have your wishes written into the will itself.

In addition to issues surrounding the literary

representative, you should be prepared to discuss who you want to benefit from the copyrights. There are two basic options here. With one option, you have a simple will that determines who gets a share in the copyright initially, but as each of those heirs dies, the deceased heirs' shares go through the deceased heir's probate, and are distributed according to the deceased share's wishes (either by will or by the laws of intestacy). Note that with this option the widow(er) of a deceased heir would likely inherit at least some interest in the copyrights, and if he or she remarried or simply willed her assets (including her interest in the copyrights) to a sibling or a friend, the interest could then be bequeathed to someone who is not your descendant.

The second option, which requires a slightly more complicated will, allows you to retain more control over who can inherit a share of the copyrights. In essence, your will would provide that all of your copyrights would be owned by a trust, with the literary representative as the trustee. The trustee would then be required to pay over the net profits to the beneficiaries, and the beneficiaries would be defined as your initial heirs, and then, as they die, their descendants will take their share. (There are a number of ways the descendants' shares can be calculated. The technicalities are beyond the scope of this book, and should be discussed with your local legal adviser.)

The terms of the trust can either be included in the will itself ("testamentary trust") or can be a separate document that creates the trust ("living trust"), which then becomes the beneficiary of your will. The choice between a testamentary trust and a living trust is beyond the scope of this book, and the decision can only be made by you, with input from an attorney who knows your local laws and your unique circumstances.

Broadly speaking, a testamentary trust may be subject to probate court supervision for the life of its existence, which is an unnecessary hassle and expense, and the terms are public knowledge, available to anyone who wants to poke around in your private business. On the other hand, a living trust offers some privacy, while having its own hassles, especially if assets are placed into the trust prior to your death. Once the trust has income-producing assets, you may need to file income tax returns for the trust, in addition to your personal income tax returns. A living trust may, in some circumstances, also restrict your ability to change your mind, at least with respect to assets you've placed in the trust, whereas a testamentary trust can be changed on a whim, by revoking or replacing your will.

What your family and representatives need to know.

While the attorney is turning the notes from your appointment into an actual will, sit down with your named literary representative and the backup literary representative(s), and make sure they really are willing to take on the responsibility. Any restrictions of authority, which you've discussed with the attorney, should also be discussed with the potential literary representatives. You may wish to write down additional instructions, simply for the literary representative's use, in your own words. It won't be legally binding, but the literary representative might find it comforting and educational. If you don't have any particularly strong feelings about how the copyrights are handled, then just let the nominees know you trust their judgment.

This is a good time to also discuss other final wishes you may have, such as those covered by a living will or health care proxy (end-of-life decisions). Generally, attorneys will include the documents for end-of-life decisions in a package price with your will, so you might as well get them done at the same time.

Note that I didn't advise you earlier to discuss your funeral plans with your attorney. Funeral arrangements don't generally go in your will, since the will isn't official until the probate court says so, which can be weeks or even months after the funeral happens. Instead, this is something to discuss with your family and representatives. If you don't talk to them, at least leave a memorandum with your preferences, or buy a prepaid funeral plan.

Obituaries are undergoing change, along with the traditional entities that published them. Let your family and representatives know if you would like a traditional obituary in a print newspaper, or if you prefer a digital version. Remember that your online friends from all across the globe aren't necessarily going to see the obituary in your local paper, so you may wish to leave instructions with respect to online friends or internet groups you would like to be notified of your passing. Many authors have a few literary/literacy-related charities, and if you have one, you may wish to have that included in your obituary for memorial donations by friends and readers.

Make sure your personal representative, literary representative and other family members know where the original of your will is. In many states, only the original, not a copy, may be presented to the court for probate. Without the original, all of your planning may be wasted. After the will is executed, you may wish to give a copy to your representatives (literary and personal), simply for their records, while keeping the original in a safe place.

Some attorneys will offer to keep the original in their offices. The attorney isn't making the offer entirely out of the goodness of his heart; he's hoping your personal representative will hire him to probate your estate. There's no obligation, and in most cases, you would probably prefer that your chosen attorney to handle the probate. Plus, it will save you the cost of a safe deposit box. It can also be more convenient than a safe deposit box, when the box is owned by just one person. In that case, when there's no joint owner of the box, the bank cannot let the personal representative into the safe deposit box until the personal representative is appointed, which can't happen until the will is retrieved, creating a catch-22, until someone goes to the probate court and gets a temporary order to access the safe deposit box. The attorney, unlike the bank, can immediately release the will to the personal representative named in the will, or file it directly with the court. On the other hand, attorneys do die or retire, sometimes without providing for a successor law firm to take over their will collection, and not all attorneys are as good as they should be at responding to requests to produce an original will for probate.

Signing the will.

When you return to the attorney's office to execute your will, you can't just sign it and pat your virtuous self on the back. You've done the hard work of figuring out what you want, so don't mess it up now.

Read the will. **The whole thing**. Don't just glance at it, and say, "yeah, yeah, whatever; where can I sign?"

Read it. If you forgot your glasses, get someone you trust to read it to you. Or ask if you can take a draft home and come back another time to sign it.

Read every single word, down to your signature line. (I wouldn't blame you if you skipped the witness attestation clauses at the end, after your signature line, which are more meaningful to the attorney and, in the future, to the probate court, than they are to you. It's not a bad idea to read those paragraphs, though. I've seen more than a few where the named witnesses didn't match the witnesses' signatures, which, in the right circumstances, could be fodder for a disgruntled heir to contest the will. The heir would probably lose in those circumstances, but even a frivolous contest can be time-consuming and expensive for the estate.)

Second, look for language, separate from the appointment of the personal representative, that a) names the literary representative and successor, b) provides an address for the literary representative and successor, c) provides a method for choosing additional successors to that literary representative, and d) establishes who gets the net profits. If you wish to limit or direct the authority of the literary representative, that information should be spelled out too. If you wanted to restrict who could inherit the shares from your original heirs, then there should be a section of the will that refers to a trust, a trustee and the beneficiaries of the trust.

Finally, if you made a gift of a copyright during your lifetime, make sure there is a specific bequest of that copyright back to that same person, in case the transfer of copyright is ever terminated by your heirs.

Chapter 11: Avoiding probate, the pros and cons

If you've made it this far (or even if you skipped here from the table of contents), you may be thinking that doing the right thing to protect your copyrights, your other assets and your heirs is too hard. There must be an easier way.

There are certainly lots of people willing to sell you an easier way. They can be found online, in financial planning workshops and in the little ads in the back of magazines with substantial numbers of retirement-age readers. Others will offer you free advice on how to avoid probate, and it's probably worth what you paid for it. They'll tell you that your cousin's boyfriend may have done something that worked just great. Or your mother's best friend managed to transfer all her assets before she died, so that there was no fuss afterwards.

The advice is not entirely wrong. It is possible to avoid probate by changing the form of ownership so that all of your assets fall in one or more categories of non-probate assets. What is generally not mentioned is that there's a price to be paid for each of the work-arounds.

Avoiding probate is one of those goals that sounds

good initially, a lot like "avoiding income taxes." But think about, and you'll see the problem. If avoiding income taxes is truly your number one goal in life, there's one foolproof way to accomplish it: quit your job, get rid of any income-producing assets, and have no income (or at least keep your income below the poverty level). You won't pay taxes, but you also won't have any money. You probably won't have a roof over your head or a car or a smartphone or a computer or anything else you might want, either.

So, before you decide that your main goal in life (and death) is to avoid probate, you should know the advantages and disadvantages of the work-arounds. There are four basic ways to avoid probate: joint title, at-death beneficiary designation, lifetime gifts, and placing all assets into a business or trust. These are all potentially valid tools in an estate plan, but they all have both benefits and drawbacks.

Joint title: It's fairly common for married couples to own assets jointly, although joint title isn't limited to spouses or to just two people. Siblings, other relatives, friends, business partners can own assets jointly, with the deceased person's share going to the survivors automatically. Real estate, motor vehicles and bank accounts are the typical examples of property owned jointly, but copyrights can also be owned jointly. In fact, books by fantasy author Terry Pratchett indicate that the copyright is jointly owned with his wife.

The advantage to putting assets into joint title is

obvious: no probate, and easy access, both before and after your death, by all persons who have a right to the assets. The biggest problem is that people are greedy. If property is owned jointly, all of the joint owners have the right to spend, transfer or sell the *entire* asset. This has the potential for being a huge problem in a country where half of all marriages end up in divorce. While there are rules against a spouse wiping out a joint bank account on the eve of a divorce, it does happen, and the remedies for getting the money back can be expensive, time-consuming and not terribly effective. What's perhaps more shocking is how often that sort of thing happens when the joint owners are parent and child. The parent adds the child's name to the account with the parent's life savings, to make it easier for the child to access the funds after the parent dies, and instead the child immediately wipes out the account, claiming his inheritance without waiting for the parent to die. There's also the risk of attachment by the joint owner's creditors. For example, an unmarried author might decide to add his sister's name to his bank account, the account where his royalties or profits are automatically deposited. The intent is that the sister, his only living relative, would then have access to the account if he died, without having to go through probate. Even if the sister is a good person, and doesn't abscond with the funds, the account could be emptied as a result of a lawsuit against the sister (*e.g.*, she caused a serious car accident, and the injured person sued her for an amount in excess of her insurance coverage). Since her name is on the account, the victim could place a lien on the account for the duration of the litigation, and if the victim won in court, he could take the monies in the account to pay the judgment.

A variation on placing assets in joint title is to keep the asset, usually an online bank account or one with ATM access, in your name, but give the password to your intended heir for immediate access after your death. The risk of theft is the same as if it were a joint account, but the account couldn't be attached by the other person's creditors. It may not accomplish your intent, either, if the financial institution learns of your death, and freezes your account. While this sort of work-around might be useful for giving your heirs access to some small amounts of emergency cash, it's not a final solution. At some point, more formal action will need to be taken to close out the account.

Life estates: Some assets can be structured so that you are the sole owner during your lifetime ("lifetime beneficiary"), and then someone else designated by you (the "contingent beneficiary") gets whatever is left at the time of your death. Copyright registration, however, doesn't have a reliable procedure for establishing this form of ownership, so this method for avoiding probate can't remove all of your assets from your estate.

Gifts: One seemingly foolproof way to avoid probate is to give your assets to your heirs during your lifetime.

The trick, of course, is in the timing. You probably don't want to be destitute, so you'll need to keep at least some assets until the last minute, and few of us know when that last minute will be.

Giving away *part* of your estate (not the whole thing) is a common estate planning technique, but it's intended to reduce estate taxes, not to avoid probate. If your estate is slightly above the estate tax threshold for your state (or the federal government), and you make a few tax-free gifts to family or friends to reduce your assets to below the threshold, then you can avoid estate taxes, while immediately benefitting the people you care about.

The problem is that you may not want to give away any or all of your money, not even to people you love. If you make the gift to avoid probate, you can't put strings on the gift. If you have the right to take it back, it's considered to still be part of your estate, so you haven't accomplished your goal of reducing your estate for tax purposes or your goal of getting rid of all assets to avoid probate.

Giving away highly valuable assets can also have some unexpected consequences if you find yourself needing long-term care in a nursing home. It's too complicated a topic, and one that's constantly evolving, to do justice to it here. The short explanation is that if you give away all of your assets, and then apply for Medicaid to pay for your nursing home expenses, you may not qualify for assistance until a certain period of time has passed. In essence, Medicaid will assume that you faked the gift just to qualify for government assistance, and will not provide that assistance during the period you should have been able to pay your own expenses if you had not given away the assets. If you've really given away the assets, though, and can't get them back, you may be stranded for a period, without access to the nursing home care that you need.

Before making a gift of copyrights, review the discussion in Chapter 8 above on gift taxes. There may be valuation issues to address, and you could trigger the need to file a gift tax return. Also, if you make a gift of one or more of your copyrights during your lifetime, make sure to include in your will a specific bequest of that copyright to that same person, in case the transfer of copyright is ever terminated by your heirs.

Business or living trust: The last way to avoid probate, the one that's advocated in most of the seminars you may see advertised, is to establish a living trust or business entity (LLC or corporation), or a combination of the two, to own all of your assets. The obvious advantage to these forms of ownership, beyond avoiding probate, is that a trust or business entity can last indefinitely, certainly as long as your copyright, never having to be probated, even as the trustees (or LLC members or corporate stockholders) and beneficiaries die and are replaced.

The drawbacks are the expense and extra paperwork during your lifetime. You will need to have a trust or business entity created, you will need to maintain the entity, you will need to file extra tax returns (probably not pay an extra tax, just pay for preparing and filing the forms) every year, and there may be additional paperwork (and therefore expense) whenever you sell any of the assets in the trust. You may also lose some income tax benefits that are limited to assets owned by individuals or married couples, rather than businesses. One problem that I've seen frequently is that the trust or business entity is created, but then the assets aren't transferred into the new entity, or only some of the assets are transferred, leaving the rest to be probated. Even if all the known assets are transferred, there can be assets that aren't known until after someone dies, such as a medical malpractice claim or other personal injury claim against the person who killed the decedent. As a result, all the work that was done to avoid probate fails to accomplish the goal of avoiding probate.

Authors and other creative types are in a unique position, where we could at least make the argument that our very existence contributes to our writing, and therefore everything we do and own is part of the business of writing. Apparently, a few risk-tolerant artists have tried this argument, placing everything they own, from their house and car and bank accounts and stock investments and groceries and clothes, along with their copyrights, into an LLC, and then claimed all of their living expenses as business expenses. The IRS was not amused. It might have avoided probate, but at the cost of angering the IRS.

If you're not trying to avoid legitimate income taxes, but merely trying to avoid probate, you could put most of your assets into a combination of entities: a living trust and a business entity, with the business entity owning the literary assets, and the living trust owning everything else. On the other hand, there are financial and time expenses for maintaining a living trust, an LLC or both, which need to be weighed against the purported benefit of avoiding probate. Whether your circumstances justify incurring the expenses is something to discuss with a legal adviser familiar with your local laws and your unique circumstances.

Another potential pitfall for a living trust or business entity is similar to the problem with outright gifts, when it comes to applying for Medicaid. Assets held in a trust or LLC might be attributed to the patient and disqualify you from Medicaid eligibility. Similarly, if you're receiving Social Security and are under the full retirement age, the money you earn on books may result in your Social Security benefits being taxable, or may reduce the Social Security payment you receive. If you anticipate possibly needing nursing home care in the next five years, or if you are receiving Social Security (either disability or retirement, and you're under the relevant full-retirement age for Social Security), you should see an estate planner, stat, and not try to handle your estate plan on your own.

Why you still need a will.

If you are relying on any of these work-arounds to avoid probate, it's still wise to have a valid will as a fail-safe. Even if you work with a professional to create a complicated estate plan, with a living trust that owns all of your assets, you'll find that the estate planner will advise you to have what's called a "pour-over" will, that pours all your assets into the trust, just in case there are any assets that weren't placed into the trust during your lifetime.

You don't know what could happen down the road. What if you write a book and publish it and forget to transfer it into joint title or into your trust or LLC? It will need to go through probate, and in the absence of a will, your wishes with respect to who gets the profits and who manages the copyright, will not be considered by the court. What if you win the lottery the day before you're run over by a truck? The lottery winnings will not have been deposited into your joint account, trust or LLC, and so they would have to go through probate. In fact, what if you're killed in a car accident that was the other driver's fault, or you died as a result of medical malpractice? The settlement or court-awarded monies will not go into your joint account, trust or LLC, but will go through probate. What if your literary representative sues someone for violation of your copyright and collects a sizeable judgment? Will that go into your joint account, trust or LLC, or will it be deemed a probate asset?

Power of attorney.

All of the work-arounds mentioned above can work in the right circumstances, although there may be unexpected negative consequences. There is one work-around that you might have heard about, that does not work at all for the purposes of avoiding probate: a durable power of attorney.

Historically, a power of attorney authorized the attorney to act only in circumstances where the person granting the power could act. In other words, if you granted someone a power of attorney, and then became mentally incapacitated, then you couldn't enter into a contract, so the power of attorney was void.

In many states, you can now grant a "durable" power of attorney. "Durable" is somewhat misleading, since the power of attorney is still limited. It will survive the mental incapacity of the person granting the power, so it's useful for someone who is still competent but is showing signs of dementia. The designated attorney can act when the dementia renders the person incompetent, but the designated attorney still *cannot* legally act after the death of the person granting the power.

There are many legitimate reasons to grant someone a power of attorney, but avoiding probate is not one of them.

Chapter 12: Conclusion

I hope that now that you've learned the basics of estate planning, and the pitfalls to watch out for, you'll find the whole topic a little less intimidating. If you've taken notes as you went through the book, you should have a reasonably complete picture of your assets, your heirs and your wishes for how your assets will benefit your heirs in the future.

Once you've had your estate planning documents drafted and signed, make a note in your calendar (or other organizational system) to review the will in three to five years. Keep in mind that you may wish to review the documents sooner, if there's a major change in your circumstances, such as a death in the family, marriage or divorce, birth of a child, relocation to another state or country, or a significant increase in your assets.

Until then, you can rest easy, knowing that you've done the best you can to protect your copyrights when you are no longer able to manage them yourself, and to minimize the potential for expensive squabbles over those copyrights.

APPENDIX I:

Sample language for nominating a literary representative

I nominate and appoint _____ as my Literary Representative [or "Literary Executor"] with respect to any rights I now possess or may hereafter possess in any literary works or literary archival materials. In the event ___ is unwilling or unable to act as my Literary Representative, then I nominate and appoint the then senior agent of _____ Literary Agency, or its successor agency, as my Literary Representative.

The Literary Representative shall have the power to make all decisions regarding the appropriate publication, republication, sale, license or any other exploitation or enforcement of any nature of any intellectual property rights I have in any literary works or materials. He shall do these things with due regard to fostering economic return without devaluing or cheapening the literary works or any intellectual property rights flowing therefrom, or in any way reflecting negatively on me or my heirs or beneficiaries.

The Literary Representative shall receive as the sole compensation for his services ten percent (10%) of any income generated by any publication, sales or other licensing arrangements that he has negotiated, payable to him upon receipt of any such income by the estate. The Literary Representative shall be reimbursed for the reasonably necessary costs of generating income from my literary works and/or literary archival materials, including but not limited to postage, copying, purchasing cover art, and pursuing or defending against legal actions arising out of my literary works.

Disclaimer

This sample language is offered for educational purposes, to assist you in understanding the basics of an estate plan for authors. It is not intended to take the place of personalized advice from a knowledgeable lawyer qualified to practice in the jurisdiction where you live and work, and does not create an attorney-client relationship. I strongly recommend consulting with a professional before implementing your estate plan to be sure that it complies with local variations in the law and is consistent with your individual circumstances.

APPENDIX II

Sample Language for Charitable bequest

I give, devise and bequeath to [name of institution] or its successor [charitable/educational institution] any and all literary archival materials in my possession at the time of my death, including but not limited to manuscript print-outs, notes, outlines, character sketches, omitted scenes, and correspondence between me and my agents, editors, publishers and readers. I direct the institution to keep the documents together whenever feasible, and if they are unable to do so, to offer them for sale as a complete collection to [define institution]. [and restrictions on transfer, publication, making available to researchers, etc.] It is my wish that they should be widely available to readers generally, as well as to researchers, whether professional academics, students or amateurs.

Disclaimer

This sample language is offered for educational purposes, to assist you in understanding the basics of an estate plan for authors. It is not intended to take the place of personalized advice from a knowledgeable lawyer qualified to practice in the jurisdiction where you live and work, and does not create an attorney-client relationship. I strongly recommend consulting with a professional before implementing your estate plan to be sure that it complies with local variations in the law and is consistent with your individual circumstances.

APPENDIX III

Memorandum for my Literary Representative

I am currently represented by a literary agent, _____, with [name of agency and contact info], whose advice has always been valuable to me, and I would encourage you to continue with this agent, or in the event of the agent's retirement, to seek three recommendations from this agent for a successor agent. My books are under contract with _____, and I have a good working relationship with my editor, _____.

OR

I have self-published the following books, which are available through ____ and _____:

[List titles and original release date or reissue date]

Additional books may be added after the drafting of this memorandum.

Disclaimer

This sample language is offered for educational purposes, to assist you in understanding the basics of an estate plan for authors. It is not intended to take the place of personalized advice from a knowledgeable lawyer qualified to practice in the jurisdiction where you live and work, and does not create an attorney-client relationship. I strongly recommend consulting with a professional before implementing your estate plan to be sure that it complies with local variations in the law and is consistent with your individual circumstances.

APPENDIX IV: More resources

I have created worksheets to guide you through collecting and organizing information for your legal professional, personal representative and literary representative. You can copy (for your use only, not for re-publication) and print them from http://www.thewritegin.blogspot.com.

For more titles by Gin Jones on the business of writing, check out my author page at Amazon.com or the bibliography in the "Planning books" tab at my blog, http://thewritegin.blogspot.com/p/planning-books.html

Other resources you may find useful include:

Lindey on Entertainment, Publishing and the Arts (LINDEY 3D keyword on Westlaw)

The Copyright Handbook, Stephen Fishman (Nolo Press)

http://www.copyright.gov

http://journal.neilgaiman.com/2006/10/important-and-pass-it-on.html

Acknowledgements

Thank you, Sarah Gregg, for your help and encouragement.

###

www.ingramcontent.com/pod-product-compliance
Lightning Source LLC
Chambersburg PA
CBHW051338170526
45166CB00002B/862